ENTREPRENUR'S ORÀCLE

WRITTEN BY HAKIM ABEL MAHERE

PREFACE

This Digital book is dedicated to all young and upcoming entreprenurs of the 21st century, this is a simplified manual of business knowledge and processes which I have gathered along my journey as an entrepreneur, in this digital book you will learn the ropes and structures of how to do business from some of the World's best Entreprenurs. In this digital book you will gain exclusive business nuggets from across the World and you will be able to understand the journey of Entrepreneurship to it's Core, I hereby pass to you this Oracle of business knowledge so that you may be enlightened and informed. This is simply a Business Manual to kick start an Entreprenurs journey and provide a navigation compus to those who want to reach their destinations in the 21st century business World.

ENTREPRENUR'S ORACLE by HAKIM ABEL MAHERE

I'm also dedicating this book to my late mother Mercy Mahere nee Rutumu, to my Wife Gertrude, to my Father Mark Mahere, My Son Mukudzeyi Mahere and my Brother Misheck Mahere.

INTRODUCTION!

The ENTREPRENEUR'S Oracle is a very different book from most of the books many people read, firstly it is digitally designed and it will have less written words, I have found not all of us entreprenurs are fond of reading too many words, we easily get bored by concentrating on these words and consuming all that jargon in all those books so I decided to create this digital book which has less words to help you through this process of business knowledge accumulation in a simplified way but richly enhancing your business acumen. This book will take you straight into the core of business and show you exactly what you need to know and understand in a simplified manner, this is a direct link to your Entrepreneurship journey, we won't waste time in here giving you an endless maze of information but we offer you an Oracle which gives you straight up Business Wisdom without compromise.

Please use this Oracle wisely and keep it close by you all the time incase you need to consult the Oracle about something.

CREATIVITY 101

Creativity is in all of us that's why we have different finger prints, no one has the same finger prints with one another even biological twins, that is where our creativity comes from we all have our unique creative juices just like our finger prints. Creativity is in our DNA we just have to discover it through our imagination, if we take time to find our creative grooves and nurture them well we can be able to find ourselves making a fortune by using our God given creative powers. Entreprenurs must be creative in all aspects of business development, creativity is the engine that runs all successful enterprises, without creativity entreprenurs are doomed in this day and age. CREATIVITY IS THE SECRET WEAPON IN EVERY ENTREPRENURS ARSENAL!

[RISKING IT ALL]

You see Elon Musk is one of the biggest Risk takers in the world of business today, imagine taking all your millions you got from a business that you nolonger own and putting all that money into business ventures that you know are still very complicated and uncertain in the business world, how many of you can take that kind of Risk? a few I guess, Musk only shows us that if you take a gigantic risk and combine it with Faith and Passion nothing will stop you! Don't be afraid to take calculated Risk.

[BE VIGILANT IN BUSINESS, A LESSON FROM BILL GATES'S MISTAKE WITH APPLE.]

I guess Bill Gates uunderestimated Apple or Was it he underestimated Steve Jobs, I would like us to get this into our heads, never underestimate your competitors! Why? because you don't always know what's in your competitors arsenal and at the same time it's always good to be underestimated! Why? because it laverages you and gives you a fair advantage.

[DON'T LIVE A SHOW OFF LIFESTYLE IT'S A TICKET TO GO BROKE]

Showing off is a fool's idea of showing the world that you have money when you actually have nothing, money doesn't exist in liabilities, money exists in assets, when you buy a $2000 dollar Nike air sneaker that's throwing away money for potential assets, but when you by $2000 dollars shares in a company or buy a piece of farming land you have increased your money and asset base, so I want us to know that showing off isn't going to make you Rich but it will make you poor, use money wisely and stop being a consumer instead become a producer and Find ways to invest your money wisely, STOP SHOWING OFF GUYS,Be humble and economic.

[GOOD CREDIT]

Never borrow money and fail to repay it, that will ultimately give you Bad Credit rating with money lenders or Banks, you won't be able to fund your projects or business once you are blacklisted, when given a loan for business purposes use it for that purpose only don't use it for the wrong reasons because if you use it foolishly you will probably fail to repay and then you will face bad Credit ratings, always have a clean Credit rating incase of the rainy days when you really need a bail out in your business. ALWAYS HAVE A GOOD CREDIT RATING.

[21st CENTURY BUSINESS AT YOUR FINGERTIPS]

The 21st century entreprenurs are probably the Luckiest and most advantaged generation of entreprenurs, with the internet in its prime and at its best, with WiFi all over, Smartphones in our hands, Social media at our disposal,IoT, App's in the world and Google, we absolutely have the world in our palms, we can do anything in real time, we can do things much easier and more smarter. What can stop us from making this world a better place, what problems can we not solve with all these technological tools in our hands, We can become anything we want to become, we can develop and implement all we need to achieve,We are blessed to be a part of this Digital and Technological Age. We have everything we need to become Wealthy and Rich. LET'S USE THESE TECHNOLOGIES TO FURTHER HUMAN KIND AMBITIONS, CREATE A BETTER WORLD AND SOLVE ALL PRESSING PROBLEMS.

[EARLY RETIREMENT FOR ASPIRING ENTREPRENURS]

In this Age and day it is nolonger viable to work your whole life in someone's company for just a pension at the end of 25 years of service to the company. If you are an aspiring entreprenur or an upcoming entrepreneur by 30 years Old you should have worked in the coo-perate world enough and you would have gained experience to run your own ventures and retire to run your own businesses, all you need to do is to sacrifice during the time you are working in a company and organise your priorities and life around your Entrepreneurship journey, have a mapped plan of where you want to be and save money and buy assets and by 30 years you are your own Boss and you have your Freedom.

[HUSTLE 24 HOUR'S A DAY AND STOP WHEN YOU ARE DONE]

Success doesn't know sleep,vacation, holiday or weekends, success needs relentless pursuit, creating and innovation has no Limits or right time, ideas can come at anytime of the day and you have to work on it, holidays are for those who have limits in their lives, weekends are for those who doesn't know the value of time over money, whenever you are awake make sure you are doing something productive and moving towards your goals, if you sleep on an idea you will loose the zeal and juice, act on it that moment that time and put it on paper, don't stop until it's over. HUSTLE ALL THE WAY,NEVER STOP AND NEVER GET TIRED,KEEP ON CHASING THE DREAM AND THE DOTS WILL CONNECT.

[YOUR PATIENCE AND ATTITUDE TOWARDS YOUR GOALS IS KEY]

PATIENCE is what separates the wantprenuers and the real entreprenurs, Rome wasn't built in one day isn't it? So is your business Start Up, you got to have patience and a never give up spirit, you got to have faith that it will work out in good time, if you are inpatient everything will go up in smoke, you have to keep the fire burning until light of day comes, Patience is key to unlocking your Empire, Patience is a skill that must be mastered by entreprenurs,but while you wait patiently don't sleep on the job,do something small everyday and add it to your dream while you wait for the right time. Attitude is what will keep you patient enough to get there, your attitude is the kingpin, it will keep you grounded and focused on the goal while you wait to strike, you must have the attitude of a winner and keep at it and go through the process. YOUR ATTITUDE AND PATIENCE ARE THE RIGHT ALLIES TO PULL YOU THROUGH THE JOURNEY.

21st CENTURY DIGITAL BUSINESS MODEL

In this Day and Age Social media has changed the way society does things, social media has changed our cultures, it has changed the way we communicate, the way we learn, it has changed the way we do business, you can't have a successful business in this age without a presents on social media platforms, you can't build a successful Brand without impacting the social media platforms, as entreprenurs it is wise to use social media platforms to our advantage when building brands, entreprenurs must have social media skills to help scale business. 21st century entreprenurs must build viable and impacting social media business models.

[FOCUS ON THE GOAL AND FINISH UP]

Entreprenurs must master the Art of finishing what they have initiated, if you embark on a project make sure you see it through to the end, finish up the game and get a winning score, finishers are winners, in business focusing on the goal is the key to finishing up what you have embarked on. If you touch 100 things at the same time nothing will be finished, nothing will materialize, you have to commit to finishing the journey, you have to dedicate your time and energy on crossing the finish line. Never allow yourself to lose steam before reaching the destination. Focus and you will Win the race, Finishing Up important priorities is the Key to achieving goals. FINISH UP WHAT YOU HAVE STARTED AND YOU ARE A WINNER.

[GOALS]

Goals are what you set as an entrepreneur to be able to achieve your plans or to be able to come up with a solution to do something, you set goals so that you can solve problems, goals are the steps we take to make things happen, to be able to achieve your goals you must track them and hunt them down, entreprenurs must set goals and execute goals, The goals you set must not be verbal only it must be written down with a pen and paper and checked every now and then to check on progress, an entrepreneur must not settle down until the set goals are achieved, to be able to hunt down your goals you must decide to take action, goals cannot be achieved without taking action, entreprenurs must learn the skill of executing set goals with precision and by so doing the set goals will be achieved, you don't just set goals and expect them to just happen without action, Take action and achieve your GOALS.

[NEVER MIND THE CRITIC'S JUST DO IT]

You see when you do something unusual and unique amongst your peers or in your society you must be ready to be criticized and vindicated, they will judge you and discourage you, the journey of an entrepreneur is full of discouragement and stereotyping from those around us, as an entrepreneur you have to fight through rough times and criticism, don't mind the naysayers, don't pay attention to the the discouragements, just close your eyes and your ears and fly. When you start something new it is going to ruffle some furthers and produce friction but don't be detered by any of that noise, just keep on going, keep on moving, keep on walking. At the end those critic's will be the ones to cheer you up and support after all is done and said, Focus on the ball and score, dont mind the obstacles just do it and make it happen.

ENTREPRENUR'S ORACLE by HAKIM ABEL MAHERE

THE ART OF MAKING MONEY

Some people make money other's make nothing, the ones who make more money have learnt the Art of making money, the ones who make nothing have not mastered the Art of making money, money is a tool to help us achieve goals and develop our lives, money is the medium of making things happen, money is created by solving problems people face, money is amassed by understanding the rules that govern it's aquisition, money is made by investing in the right things, money is attracted to those who know where to put their money and grow it. Those who make less money or no money at all lack the knowledge and principles of growing money, those who don't have money lack financial literacy skills, the difference separates the two. Entreprenurs must learn the Art of making money because making money is an Art.

[IT'S ALL IN THE MINDSET]

If you see yourself as an entrepreneur and you just think about success without taking any action then forget about being an entrepreneur and forget about success, many people spend a lot of hours thinking and daydreaming about success but without any tangible action taken, then there are those people who are fired up at the beginning of a project and actually do something and push a little bit and then suddenly they let go, they just stop and they give up, the fire in them just dies and boom everything is gone, these kind of people we call them wantprenuers, they just want things but they don't want to face the consequences and challenges of building a business, then we have entreprenurs who are the game changers, they go out there and achieve what they set out to achieve and these are the few ones, the small population that never give up and as an entrepreneur you should be in that small population that never gives in that is where the money is. Your Mindset towards your goal is what puts you where you will be in the population, your mindset is the key to making it to the top of the top of the foodchain, Success is all in your mindset, if you are in the right set of mind you can be in the league of the Wealthy without any doubts. Have the right mindset as an entrepreneur and you are on your way to the Big Boys club.

ENTREPRENUR'S ORACLE by HAKIM ABEL MAHERE

[GET OUT OF THE COMFORT ZONE]

Never be too comfortable with mediocrity if your are an entrepreneur, don't be satisfied with being average, shoot for the sky and never look back on comfort, comfort is a cancer that will destroy an entrepreneur's dream, think outside of the box , don't live in a cacoon, jump out of the comfortable corner you are Locked in, it doesn't have any benefit feeling too safe and secure, if you get too comfortable as an entrepreneur then you are out and done, to stay relevant in the game you have to be uncomfortable with the status quo, fly out of the comfort zone and live on the edge, comfort will kill your passion and creativity, the more you are comfortable the more your mind goes into slumber, Be uncomfortable with comfort, go out there and define yourself, curve yourself out of stone into a new and beautiful peice of Art. Don't entertain comfort, embrace risk and uncertainty because everything you have ever wanted is on the other side of fear. DON'T BE TOO COMFORTABLE with life , never settle. COMFORT IS A DREAM KILLER.

[SCALABILITY]

In business being able to scale your business up is the ultimate goal of every entreprenur, scaling your business will increase your customer base and expand your business, as an entrepreneur you must find ways to scale up your business in a cost effective way without compromising the business cashflow. You must know your market in and out to be able to achieve the desired results, you must know your customers and understand what they need and know who your customers

are, you need to create products that will concur with your scaling plan, business can only grow if you implement the best scaling model for the market you are targeting. Scalability is simply expanding your horizons in your business and growing your market base.

[ROME WAS NOT BUILT IN A DAY]

Some of us have heard the saying that Rome wasn't Built in a day and that's damn true, great thing's take time to build, small things happen fast and they die a quick death also, entreprenurs must know that building a business or a brand just doesn't happen overnight it's a process and that process takes a large amount of time and effort, you can't expect a business to be successful in a month or a year, if you are building something great you must be ready for some dry spells otherwise you will be disappointed, stop daydreaming about these get Rich quick schemes there is nothing like that, you have to stay committed and dedicated to achieve the ultimate goal. Great thing's are built over time, great thing's require great effort and great resilience, to be successful as an entrepreneur you have to go through the process of building and that process is invertible, there are no shortcuts in business, roll your sleeves and get down to work, never stop working keep on building. It will happen in good time. Building a business is a journey of a thousand miles, to reach your destination you have to go all out and face the challenges ahead and conquer all the obstacles along the way. Nothing happens overnight.

[DON'T WISH IT HAPPENS MAKE IT HAPPEN]

Most people spend their time wishing things would happen as they wish! You can't seat all day and daydream that things will turn out for the better without taking a step towards your dream, you can't just hope that it will happen without making it happen, you are the man in the arena and you are the man who must make it happen, no one will make it happen for you, go out there and take what is yours, take a step and reach out to your dream, make it happen by doing something about it, Run as fast as you can towards what you desire, simply wishing without taking action will yield nothing , just go out there and make it happen, it's you who makes it happen. Take bold steps and be courageous, move towards your dream and execute it.

[9 COMMANDMENTS FROM THE ORACLE TO YOU]

The Oracle gives you these 9 commandments to achieve your goals, if you follow the above commandments they will guide you through your journey, these commandments if applied in the correct manner and if practiced well it will make things happen for you without doubt, write them down in your journal or piece of paper and practice them all the time and you will be delivered to your dream. Master these 9 commandments and you are on your way to success and greatness.

[BUILDING YOUR BRAND]

Every brand is a story, brands are stories, to build a great brand you must have a great story, your products depend on the story behind your brand, a brand is a name that is built to sale and impact people's lives, entreprenurs must build their brands by creating great products and solutions for their customers, a great product and a great story will give you an exceptional Brand . Your Brand is the heartbeat of your business model, an example of a great brand name is the Virgin Group by Richard Branson, Branson created his brand by using his life stories to impact his business. Connect the story of your life and your product and a great brand will evolve from that combination.Build your brand without Limits, express yourself through your products, build your brand through your passion and creativity. START YOUR BRAND ON THE RIGHT FOOTING WITH THE RIGHT STORY.

[THE POWER OF KNOWLEDGE AND INFORMATION]

Knowledge is the new currency in this 21st century and Information is the most valuable asset in this 21st century, those who are constantly learning and relearning will be the one's to lead us into the Future, those who have fresh information will be the winners, in this age if you are an entrepreneur you have to learn something new everyday, you have to have a hunger for knowledge and information, that's the only way to make it to the top of the Maslow's Hierarchy Pyramid.The one's who stop learning and accumulating knowledge are going to lose everything because everything is going to be changing everyday and at a faster pace. In order to move along with the changes and developments in the business world an entreprenur is required to be on a constant learning and reading mode.

To build an empire that spans generations entreprenurs must cultivate a culture of reading and learning new thing's everyday without limit. KNOWLEDGE AND INFORMATION IS THE KEY TO THE FUTURE.

[WHERE TO PUT YOUR MONEY AS A YOUNG ENTREPRENUR]

The most valuable investment you can ever make as an aspiring entrepreneur or as a young entrepreneur is to invest in yourself, You are the man in the Arena, you are the brain's behind all your creations that's why it's so important to invest heavily in you, once you invest in yourself then you have increased your Net-worth more than double, invest in your health, invest in your self education, invest in your time, invest in your skills. The more you invest in valuable books and articles the more you grow your horizons, read books, Read article's and you have done yourself a great favour, go to serminars, listen to podcasts, associate yourself with like-minded people, all these mentioned activities will lead you in the right direction to a greater future.

Don't invest in stupid thing's like clothes, expensive drinks, expensive lifestyle, invest in your abilities and your future. PUT YOUR MONEY WHERE YOUR MOUTH IS!

ENTREPRENUR'S ORACLE by HAKIM ABEL MAHERE

[DON'T BE BRAINWASHED BY YOUR DAY JOB]

Having a day job is a dream of many, why ? because they where conditioned that way and they where taught that it's the only way to a better life, the issue here is that realistically a job is not going to give you the freedom and independence you want in life it's just going to give you a little bit of Comfort and your employer's will make sure you stay in that comfort zone, you see if you want to make it to the top of the food chain you have to understand that a Day job will not take you there, you have to find and create multiple sources of income, some side hustles to expand your horizons, if you get comfortable with employment, you will end up being a 9 to 5 Slave, you will never taste your freedom because then you would have been brainwashed by your Job, you will be so afraid to take the bold step towards your freedom, get out of the rat race and open your own path, blaze your own trail and see where it leads you. Unchain your mind from the job syndrome. Work out something that represents you and your ideas. STOP DEPENDING ON A DAY JOB, EMBRACE YOUR ENTREPRENEURSHIP SPIRIT.

[THE POWER OF INNOVATION]

In any business in this digital age, innovation must be at the core of any project,Idea or creation. Innovation is the Midas touch in whatever product or service you want to give to consumers,. Innovation is the king pin to any business succeeding, without innovation there is no life, what is innovation? Innovation is the ability to create a better way to do something or to change the way things are done and do them in a smarter way, innovation is finding better ways to get something done in a more convenient way. Innovation is the result of creativity. There is power in innovation, the future is created by innovation, without innovation we can't go into the Future, Innovation steers the world into a

an imaginary future that we can only imagine today. In this 21st century entreprenurs must dig deep into their souls and minds and come up with innovative solutions for the future and our current problems. INNOVATION IS KING, INNOVATION IS THE VEHICLE THAT TAKES US INTO THE FUTURE.

ENTREPRENUR'S ORACLE by HAKIM ABEL MAHERE

[WHAT DO YOU CHOOSE TO DO WITH WHAT'S IN YOUR HAND]

What kind of entreprenur are you, what do you do with your time, what are you doing with that Tablet or smartphone in your Hands, do you realise what you are holding in your hands, what are you doing with it, what are you gaining from the Data that you are using on the internet, Data is now more valuable than Oil according to some experts, Be a wise entreprenur, use that smartphone to expand your horizons and business, use that Data to gain more knowledge and information, use that tablet as a business tool, stop wasting data on stupid thing's like watching pornography,cheap entertainment, downloading stupid things on the internet, Stop it, use your time and resources wisely, use what is in your hands to achieve your goals and dreams. Improve your life by creating value from the resources you are holding in your hands, open your eyes and realise that wealth is created by the way you use the resources that you have at your disposal, [what is it that you are holding in your hands] (in the words of my mentor Dr S.Masiyiwa) Use the internet wisely, use your social media platforms wisely,use the gadgets in your hands wisely, start a small business, start a blog, read books on your tab, connect with the right people, network with the correct people,open a youtube channel with that smartphone, enroll and take a course or learn a new skill using that Data and with that you can steer your ship towards your dreams. USE YOUR TIME AND RESOURCES WISELY, USE WHAT YOU ARE HOLDING IN YOUR HANDS IN A SMART WAY AND CREATE WEALTH.

[DO SOMETHING WITH YOUR IDEAS DON'T JUST EXIST]

Whenever you get an idea write it down and begin working on it , don't just have ideas without acting on them, take action on your ideas, don't wait for it to be perfect because it will never be perfect, just get down to work and work it out, you will get the answers along the way, ideas are like a seed in your brain if watered and taken care of they will grow and produce fruit's, ideas are seeds that God plants in our minds time and again but it is up to you the entreprenur to make sure that the seed germinates and grows into a fully grown plant. Jump into the arena and get into action with your Idea, stop procrastinating and make it happen in that moment before the flame dies, to keep the flame burning do something about your idea, in this 21st century the world needs more ideas from entreprenurs to solve all the problems around us or to at least correct the wrong things we have done in the past. Entreprenurs must work on the ideas as soon as possible, before someone else thinks of the same thing. GO INTO ACTION WITH YOUR DREAMS.

[WORK SMARTER DON'T JUST WORK]

The entreprenur of the 21st century must not just work for the sake of working, they must work smarter with precision, working smarter is not about spending the whole being busy over nothing, there is a difference between being busy and being productive, if you work smarter you will get more production with minimum labour and minimal effort, but if you just get busy without carefully organising your activities around your work you will put in maximum effort and labour and still get minimum production. Working smarter is the ability to find the most efficient and effective way to execute a task at hand without overworking yourself. Don't just run around without a clearly defined process of doing your work, create a process that has minimal input and maximum production outcome and then you know you are working smart. Entreprenurs must cultivate some smart working skills to achieve greatness. WORK SMARTER AND ACHIEVE MORE WITHOUT STRUGGLE.

[PROTECT YOUR BUSINESS SECRET'S]

Never make the mistake of talking about your business Secret's, Don't go around telling people your business Secret's everywhere you meet people, talk about your idea and business but don't reveal your business methods and techniques, that is what runs your business engine, it is for you to know only, don't reveal everything about your operations, you must know what to say and what not to say, keep your business Secret's safe, think about Coca Cola not many people are aware of the original Coke recipe, it is a well guarded secret and Coca Cola has kept it under wraps for decades that's what we call protecting your business interests, keep what is most important about your operations under wraps. Don't reveal all you do about your business it's what keeps the business intact. KEEP YOUR BUSINESS TOP SECRETS SAFE AND SECURE FROM THE WOLVES.

[BE DIFFERENT, DON'T FOLLOW THE CROWD]

If you do what everyone is doing then you are not a 21st century entreprenur, you are a stone age or iron age entreprenur, in this age you have to find your uniqueness, you have to dig deep into your brain cells and bring out your Creative powers and do things in a new way that has never been seen before, don't follow what everyone is doing, don't follow the trends, be the trend setter, travel with the less travelled road or at best open a new path that has never been travelled, blaze a new trail, curve a new niche. In order to be in possession of what others wish for you have to do what they hate to do, do what they won't do and you will be the leader, unfamiliar things attract the attention of the masses, unfamiliar territory possess special treasures. Find your own way, Sail through unchartered waters and you will find endless possibilities and opportunities. Be different from the rest and you be the best among the rest. BEING DIFFERENT IS THE KEY TO ENDLESS POSSIBILITIES, DO WHAT THE REST WON'T DO AND YOU WILL HAVE WHAT THEY WISH FOR!

[BE PREPARED FOR OPPORTUNITIES ALL THE TIME]

Opportunities always favour the prepared, never allow opportunity to pass you by while you're asleep, entreprenurs must be ever ready for opportunities, opportunities come at any given time without any notice, be ready all the time, work on your projects now and again even though you haven't hit the target, you must always be on the lookout for your opportunity, time is never on our side, things are constantly changing, it is wise for an entrepreneur to be ready and set to go at any given moment, if you miss your opportunities then you are not ready to be at the top of the league, always practice and improve your self now and again. BE READY FOR YOUR OPPORTUNITY WHEN IT COMES ALONG, NEVER MISS YOUR CHANCE, GRAB YOUR OPPORTUNITY WITH PRECISION.

SUCCESS [WHAT IT IS & WHAT IT IS NOT]

Success reflects it's self in the lives you have changed and touched through your activities, success is what we do with what we have to change this world, success is going out there to make an impact in other people's lives, people define success in many ways, to others success is achieving whatever goal you have set for yourself, but to an entrepreneur success should be about changing lives and impacting lives through solving problems affecting our societies and communities. Success is not about the cars that you have in your garage, it's not about owning private jets, success is all about making this world a better place through life changing initiatives. Having a lot of money in the bank is not success, giving homeless people a place to stay and a reason to live is success, your success as an entreprenur must stem from a much higher purpose than yourself. BE A SUCCESS THROUGH CHANGING OTHER PEOPLE'S LIVES AND MAKING THIS WORLD A BETTER PLACE.

CHALLENGE YOUR LIMITATIONS

The only way you can grow as an entrepreneur is by challenging yourself and setting for yourself scary but attainable goals, climb that mountain and reach for the summit, don't be afraid of what you don't know, work out the Solutions and challenge your limitations, Education is a lifetime process, you can never stop learning because life in it's original form is a constant learning process, Challenge yourself in all aspects of your business life and personal life, go for that bunjee jumping adventure, go for that skydiving trip, go for that safari hunting trip, just go out there and conquer your fears, go out there and define yourself and explore the world, motivate yourself with your challenges and failures because they are the best teachers. CHALLENGE YOURSELF AND REACH FOR YOUR DREAMS.

[NO LIMITS]

There are no limits in an entrepreneur's journey, if you limit your horizons you are limiting your success, open your eyes and see don't just exist, organise yourself and prosper, the journey of Entrepreneurship is not for the faint hearted it's for the crazy one's, you have to be insane at some point if you are an entrepreneur, kick ass and break your barriers, never stop hustling, keep it coming. Those who have no limits can have everything they desire on this earth. Stop limiting yourself, be open minded, be free like a bird, fly above the limiting sky's. Never settle for less, be the best at what you do, create the best and hope for the best. Never mind the brick walls in front of you, make something with those bricks, create something with those bricks,paint something on the brick wall and invite people to come and pay and watch your work of art on that brick wall. NEVER LIMIT YOUR LIFE BE CREATIVE AND INNOVATIVE AND BE UNLIMITED.

[YOU ARE UNIQUE]

What deferentiates you as an entrepreneur is your uniqueness in every aspect of your journey, in order for you to achieve your goals you have to cultivate a culture of doing things in a more uncommon way, you have to do things in a more creative way, your level of creativity is the key to becoming unique. Never be satisfied with mediocrity, keep on improving your skills everyday and be open to change, to be different you must develop the skill of learning and relearning thing's,the world is changing at a faster pace everyday and that requires entreprenurs to develop special skills and cultivate a special kind of mindset that carter's for the future. In this age you can't be thinking using a 19th century mindset, you have to understand the importance and value of the microchip, the microchip has totally changed the way we live and do things in this age and that requires a unique mindset. BE DIFFERENT,BE UNIQUE,BE AUTHENTIC,BE ORIGINAL,BE YOU.

[YOU ARE YOUR OWN COMPETITION]

The only competition you have right now is inside you,look in the mirror and what you see there is your competition, don't worry about other people and all the external forces that you come across, they are not the competition, the competition is in your head, don't compete with the wrong thing's, compete with yourself, stop wasting time thinking about the petty competition you see in your eyes and imagination, walk the talk and act the part, don't mind what others are saying, mind your own business, you are the competition, there is no better competition than the competition inside of you. STOP

COMPETING WITH THE WRONG THINGS, CORRECT YOURSELF, INSPECT YOURSELF AND CORRECT YOUR MINDSET AND WITH THAT YOU HAVE BEATEN ALL THE COMPETITION.

[TAKING THE FIRST STEPS]

Idea's are everywhere, people are constantly coming up with ideas everyday,every minute ideas are all over,the problem is that 90% of the ideas people come up with never make it through the idea stage,they never make it to the concept stage, action never takes place,taking the first steps towards bringing an idea to life is the hardest thing for young and upcoming entreprenurs, a few ideas end up in the Arena where the battle is happening, the bulk of the idea's never make it out of the brain's.The executing part of an idea is the hardest part, to be able to to execute entreprenurs must cultivate the art of executing small tasks at a time and learn to achieve a small goals at a time every day this will eventually add up and help achieve the desired results of executing the bigger goals,if you want to eat an elephant you have to eat it one piece at a time or you find others who can help you to eat it and share the spoils, that's how idea's come into life, for your idea's to evolve into reality you have to join the puzzle one piece at a time, it is possible and it can be done.GET INTO ACTION WITH YOUR IDEAS AND EXECUTE WITH TACT AND PRECISION.

[GET OUT OF THE RAT RACE]

In the 21st century we call it the rat race, many people are programmed to go to school,pass in school find a job and go to work for the rest of their lives, in this age and changing times that kind of program won't work, it worked in the industrial age but not in this digital age, in this age everything is going digital and everything will be automated, being employed will be a thing of the past with robots,Apps and IoT in the work places it will be a different world from what the kids in the Education systems are being taught, entreprenurs of today must embrace the changes in the system's and create new jobs and new careers for the 21st cence, If you want to be the next millionaire get out of the rat race, you can't work in a private company and expect to make it into the bbillionaires club, go out there and define yourself through your creativity and your skills, with that you will be in the process of building a great life in business. Start from the ground up and provide great service to the world. The world needs new thinkers, we need new methods, we need new kind of jobs, let's do away with the old and embrace the future, create your own path and explore new opportunities and challenges.

[PERSONALISE YOUR BRAND]

In this age your brand is your business, branding is the most important thing in any business, the story of your brand is what increases your sale's and put your business in the right position in any market. As an entrepreneur you must create a brand that resonates with your life story or bring in a story that resonates with the product you have or the service you are offering. When you are selling products you must sell them in combination with a fantastic story, because people buy great stories, people are inspired by greàt stories, give them what they want and they will give you what you want, the story you present to the world is what will build your Brand!
GIVE PEOPLE A GREAT STORY AND YOU WILL REAP GREAT REWARDS.

[TAKE CHARGE OF YOUR LIFE]

Be in charge of your life, be incharge of your priorities, be incharge of your goals,be incharge of your journey,be incharge of your aspirations, never let anyone hold the pen and write your life story for you, never allow society to dictate how you live your life or how you lead your life, as an entrepreneur you must be the Lead actor in the movie of your life, you must be the director and producer of your life story, focus on your strengths and experiences. Fight your fights, ruñ your race, create your reality, give yourself time to reflect and time to be grateful for everything that you have, because only then will you be content and only then will you be in control of your own life. Create alone time to meditate and think deeply, because then you will understand the true you and take charge of your life. BE IN CHARGE IF YOUR MINDSET

[CHOOSE YOU AND PUT YOURSELF FIRST]

The best choice in an entreprenur's life is to choose yourself and your ideas first, put your ideas as the number one priority when in comes to your Entrepreneurship journey, never put yourself as a second choice, you are the first choice, own your decisions, run your own business, mind your own business. Never spend your whole life pushing somebody else's Dreams and aspirations while ignoring yours. Your dreams and aspirations are the number one goals to achieve. Make the choice everyday to look inside you and release your dreams to the universe, once you release your inner intentions the universe will not stand in your way, it will open up the way for you and let you pass. The best choice is to start your own things while you still can, you are the man, go on and choose YOU.

[UNLEASH YOUR GREANESS]

Great minds are the ones that will take this world forward into the future, release your greatness, take the lead and show the world the way of the future. Inspire everyone who crosses your path and leave a mark in their memories, lead from where you are, do great things, speak greatness and inspire your community, inspire your society, never settle for less, do the things that many are afraid to do, do what others think is impossible and inspire a generation. Open up your greatness, bring out those great ideas and act on them and change the course of mankind, with that you will leave this world a better place. As an entrepreneur you must strive for greatness, accumulate knowledge and wisdom and use it to change people's lives. BE GREAT AND MAKE THIS WORLD A BETTER PLACE.

[BE CREATIVE AND INNOVATIVE]

The 21st century entreprenurs must cultivate and develop Creative and innovative skills, we can nolonger keep on reinventing things but we can still innovate and develop better solutions, there is so much we can do with a simple stone or nail, we can create more value or create new models of things, innovation is all about adding something or removing something+-, creativity is all about imagination and curiosity, with these skills entreprenurs can be àble to solve many of humanities problems. The entreprenurs of today must be always on a constant learning mode, this will help in keeping up with changes in the world, creativity and innovation demands that we keep on learning and relearning thing's. DON'T REINVENT THE WHEEL INNOVATIVE AND CREATE NEW WAYS OF DOING .

[BE INTERESTING AND ATTRACTIVE]

In this century people give more attention to what is popular and trending, entreprenurs of today must build attractive products and services, to get attention from the consumer's you must have an interesting thing's going on, attractiveness brings more business, give people a reason to smile and they will give you attention, to attract money you must be interesting, to get attention you must do things in uncommon ways, people are not interested in the ordinary, they are interested in the extra ordinary, money will always follow the exciting and the interesting patterns in society. ATTRACTIVENESS AND INTERESTING ARE THE KEYS TO NON STOP CASHFLOW. ATTENTION IS GAINED BY BEING ATTRACTIVE AND INTERESTING.

[KNOW YOUR MARKET KNOW YOUR CUSTOMER]

A 21st century entreprenur must be able to point out Who their customer really is, you have to know your market in depth and width, understand the needs of your targeted market, every entreprenur today must know exactly Who they are making the product for, understand the mindset of your customer and convince the whole target market why they should choose your product or service. Do not target everyone, not everyone is your customer, know exactly who you are targeting, people have different needs and different incomes, because of that difference you must make sure you are offering the service to the right people.
KNOW YOUR TARGET, KNOW WHO YOUR CUSTOMERS ARE?

[KNOW YOURSELF, UNDERSTAND WHO YOU ARE]

If you are an entrepreneur you must understand yourself and know what you are made of, you must know your DNA, look for the signs and symptoms of an entreprenur in you, by knowing and understanding yourself it puts you in a better space and positions you in the correct place. It must excite you at every stage and you must love what you do, as an entrepreneur you must understand yourself for the sake of growth and development, without knowing yourself better the chances of winning are below average. Take heart in the thing's you do, have a connection with your business. If your blood is screaming entreprenur you can feel it inside without doubt, know yourself and learn to.

KNOW YOURSELF AND FIND FIND YOUR GROOVE .

[THE POWER OF PROBLEMS]

Problems are the key to any Innovation or invention, the necessity is derived from problems, without problems there is no progress or development, the things we admire today came out of the problems faced in the past, if you are an entrepreneur you must always be on the look out for problems to solve, problem solving is a billion dollar business, never run away from problems, embrace the problems and role your sleeves and get to work, the obstacles we see along the way are the things that make a few man Rich, Problem solving is the most important skill required in an entrepreneur's arsenal, if you are not encountering any problems know that there is a huge mistake happening somewhere along the lines. Problems solved is equals to more money in the bank. Problems are powerful because in them we find new ways, problems are the creator's of great wealth. Next time when you encounter problems don't get angry, just smile and Develop a solution, you never know you might be the next big thing.

PROBLEM SOLVED EQUALLS SUCCESS!

[DO THAT WHICH YOU LOVE]

Your life as an entrepreneur is like a canvas, on this canvas you must paint the picture that you want to see in your in your life, paint that picture in the best possible way, Whatever comes into your mind take action and do something about it, do the things you want see done, change the thing's you want to see changed, open the path that you want to travel in, curve yourself into that sculpture that you want to put up in front of the world. Play the games that you want to play and go where you want to go, be with who you want to be with. Use your time to do the thing's that matter in your life, follow you passions, fulfilment comes from doing that which you love, live your life without limits, explore and never settle, experiment and expirience in whatever excites you.

DO THE THINGS THAT EXCITES EVRYDAY AND NEVER SETTLE.

[TIMELESS WEALTH PRINCIPLES]

For the 21st century entreprenur it's rule number one to master wealth principles, the accumulation of wealth is a process that is governed by principles, and to be able to build Wealth one must grasp these principles.

Principle(1) Be a fast follower

(2)Build relationships and connections

(3)Build a great reputation,your reputation is important

(4)Never stop learning, learn everyday and read

(5)Be open to change and be open minded

(6) Don't follow the crowd be different, be original

(7)Work smart and logically.

(8)Take care of your Health, your health is important

[IT'S NOT ALL ABOUT THE MONEY]

When it comes to business money is secondary, money should not be the only reason to get into business, there must be something deeper than that , something like the development and advancement of humankind, we must strive for something greater than ourselves or money, money should come as a result of our service to humankind, when starting a business the most important thing is to serve mankind to the best of our abilities, money will follow solution bearers, money is attracted to problem solvers, help people realise their aspirations and inturn the universe will reward you for that , if your business or organisation is all about the money then that business is doomed, a business with no vision for the people is a failure, money should be a reward for the efforts and service. Money is less important in a great organisation, but vision and mission is the most important things, Value is what business should give and then money will follow.

MONEY IS SECONDARY PURPOSE IS PRIMARY.

[CULTIVATE THE CULTURE OF READING]

Books are everything in an entrepreneur's journey, if you are to make it in the business world you need to cultivate the habit of reading book's every now and then, book's are the essence of every entreprenurs journey, without any delay, start reading now and it will broaden your horizons, reading will open a whole new world for you, reading will give you an unlimited life, reading will take you from the bottom to the top of your game. You should love book's and it will change your world, love reading and it will open your eyes.

CULTIVATE THE CULTURE OF READING

[YOUR WORDS AND THOUGHTS ARE KEY TO SUCCESS]

Be mindful of your thoughts and words, they are the keys to whatever happens in the journey of life, think before you open your mouth, Whatever occupies your mind all the time shall come to reality, your words are powerful and your thoughts shape your actions, Master your mind and control your thoughts, Cultivate good thoughts and teach your mouth to say positive thing's, if you Cultivate good thoughts and good deeds your actions will help you grow better. What you think always is what you believe, what you say will surely become, words usually become your reality, never allow your thoughts and mouth to control you, you must take charge because what you think and say will manifest.

THINK GOOD THOUGHTS AND SAY GOOD THINGS.

www.ingramcontent.com/pod-product-compliance
Lightning Source LLC
Chambersburg PA
CBHW031601210526
45464CB00003B/1378